THE HURT, THE FORGIVEN,
THE BROKEN, AND THE STRUGGLES

of Them All

Forgiveness

JEMILAT OLOLADE SIJU

Forgiveness

Praise for *Forgiveness* by Jemilat Ololade Siju

What an amazing read. Where do I start? This has blessed me so much so that I literally read it twice because I first had my life turned inside out, then had to make sure I understood it properly so that I can start putting it into practice. It helped me to see a lot of things from the other person's perspective with myself in mind. And I would love to receive grace so I guess I should start dishing it out. It won't be something I can instantaneously implement since it's not easy to change one's lifestyle but it sure is my meal plan for this part of my life. God bless you and continue to use you to speak life!

—Taiye Adesanya

I feel so blessed to have read this very practical book. Not only does Ololade Siju carefully address the dilemmas faced by those who are hurt, she also shines light on what true forgiveness is. She highlights ways to check yourself to know if you have truly forgiven and guides you down a path of reconciliation. I would highly recommend this book to anyone, regardless of age or status that is struggling while holding on to any type of hurt.

—Chidiebere Eze, BSC, PharmD

FORGIVENESS: THE STRUGGLE
by Jemilat Ololade Siju
Published by Loladesiju Ministries;
www.loladesiju.com
20, LORELEI ROAD, WEST ORANGE, NJ 07052
IG: @LIFESOURCERELATIONSHIPS / www.loladesiju.com

This book or parts thereof may not be reproduced in any form, stored in a retrieval system, or transmitted in any form by any means—electronic, mechanical, photocopy, recording, or otherwise—without prior written permission of the publisher, except as provided by United States of America copyright law.

Unless otherwise noted, all Scripture quotations are taken from the King James Version of the Bible.

Scripture quotations marked NIV are taken from the Holy Bible, New International Version®, NIV®. Copyright © 1973, 1978, 1984, 2011 by Biblica, Inc.™ Used by permission of Zondervan. All rights reserved worldwide.www.zondervan.com. The "NIV" and "New International Version" are trademarks registered in the United States Patent and Trademark Office by Biblica, Inc.™

Copyright © 2020 by Jemilat Siju
All rights reserved

Visit the author's website at IG: @ LIFESOURCERELATIONSHIPS / www.loladesiju.com

International Standard Book Number: 978-1-7352282-1-1
E-book ISBN: 978-1-7352282-2-8

While the author has made every effort to provide accurate internet addresses at the time of publication, neither the publisher nor the author assumes any responsibility for errors or for changes that occur after publication. Further, the publisher does not have any control over and does not assume any responsibility for author or third-party websites or their content.

20 21 22 23 24 — 987654321
Printed in the United States of America

CONTENTS

Acknowledgments xi

Preface xiii

Introduction xvii

Chapter 1: The Struggle Within 1

Chapter 2: Dealing with
   Difficult People 12

Chapter 3: How Do I Heal? 21

Chapter 4: Working Through It 29

Chapter 5: Resolve or Evade 49

Chapter 6: To Forget or Not to Forget . . . 55

ACKNOWLEDGMENTS

I would like to thank the Lord Jesus, my Lord and Savior for an opportunity to be used by Him to pen His thoughts into a message to the world. Thank You, Lord. I feel so honored that You chose me to convey Your message to Your people. I am eternally grateful.

To my husband, my support system, my cheerleader, my prophet, and friend. I am so grateful for all you have been to me. Thank you for investing so much into me spiritually. May God honor you always in Jesus mighty name. Amen. To my children, Deborah, David and Michael, mummy loves you.

My sincere gratitude to my spiritual leaders Dr. Amos and Esther Fenwa. God bless you.

A huge thanks to Mrs. Taiye Adesanya and Ms. Chidiebere Eze for offering up their time to help proof the first draft of this book. I am most grateful.

To all my ladies, who have been a blessing to my life, I am humbled by your generosity always. To my church family, Holy Ghost Christian Center New Jersey, I love you and I value you all. God bless you.

PREFACE

When the Lord Jesus laid this book on my heart almost five years ago, He led me through certain experiences while He taught me about forgiveness. I understand what it means to be hurt by others. I understand how excruciatingly painful it is when the people you least expect hurt you deeply. Although I consider myself a people person, I have had my fair share of struggles when it comes to relating with others and keeping the peace. In this book, I would like to share with you my biggest struggles around forgiveness and maintaining healthy relationships thereafter.

There was a young woman that I loved so much and wanted the best things for in life. She became friends with a young man, whom I equally loved and wished well. During the course of their relationship, I may have unknowingly offended both of them. They were upset and began speaking ill of me

Forgiveness: The Struggle

between themselves. Neither of them thought to tell me about it. One fateful day, I needed some information from the young woman's phone and unintentionally ran across a message trail between them. My heart broke at their use of some horrible words and qualifiers. Not only did I love these individuals, I thought they loved me too. I felt betrayed and found myself struggling to forgive for almost a year. I tried hard to shake off the feeling and the hurt, as I knew that as God's child, I had a mandate to forgive and let go. But boy, was it difficult.

I am forever grateful for the Holy Spirit. During that challenging season, He kept me and reminded me to forgive and let go, especially if I wanted to be blessed. On many occasions, I thought I had forgiven but whenever I received a text from them, heard their voices or saw them, my skin would crawl, and I would relive the hurt all over again. While driving to church once, the Holy Spirit said to me, "You have not forgiven yet" and I said "Yes, I have" and He responded saying "No, you haven't, and you must forgive so you can fulfil your purpose and be whom I have called you to be." That day, I opened my heart and said, "Lord, I choose to truly forgive" and decided that I would interact with the lady despite the physical discomfort I experienced whenever I was in her presence. To God be the glory, it has been a few years since that incident and I can honestly say I am in a place of peace with not just the lady, but also the gentleman. Having been through this experience I learned that the verbal words, "I forgive you," is not merely enough, but a starting point to a journey that only the Spirit of God can take you through.

To those of you who love freely and give selflessly to others, especially in cases where people do not value and appreciate you, I encourage you to keep going strong. Remember that you LOVE, and you GIVE only for the Holy Spirit. God is always with you. He sees your heart.

INTRODUCTION

It is amazing how people tell you to forgive whenever you get hurt by another person. They say it like it's easy to forgive, like they know how much or how deeply you are hurting. They seem to lose sense of the depth of your pain and suffering. It is like they are asking you to roll over and be a fool and let someone else get away with toying with your emotions. It becomes really hard to let go of the hurt, how much more to forget the offense. No wonder many of us get stuck with pain and in pain, sometimes even for years. In an attempt to protect ourselves, we build a defense and shut out any positive voice of reason. Whenever there is hurt or pain, there is this graphic breakdown of the negative aspects of the event, making it much more difficult to let go. The enemy gives you reasons why you must not forgive, reasons why you are right, reasons why you should hold on to the hurt and remain just where you are as compared to being free.

Forgiveness however is a gift, a special gift from God. A gift we have received freely from Him due to the sacrifice Jesus made on Calvary. He died that we may receive life and liberty, despite the fact that we do not deserve it. His love for us drove Him to the cross and He paid a price that has no measure, the price that has granted us access freely into His presence and into the abundance of all good things He has in store for us.

> For God so loved the world, that he gave his only begotten Son, that whosoever believeth in him should not perish, but have everlasting life.
> —JOHN 3:16

The same way God forgave and continues to forgive us every day despite the fact that we do not deserve it, His expectation is that we do the same when others are concerned. In the Lord's Prayer, "He said He will forgive us only if we forgive others."

> And forgive us our debts, as we forgive our debtors.... But if ye forgive

Introduction

> not men their trespasses, neither will
> your Father forgive your trespasses.
> —MATTHEW 6:12, 15

Forgiveness is not only a gift from God to us; it is also a gift we give to others and to ourselves. Forgiveness is power, freedom, and liberty. Every time we choose to forgive, we bless ourselves and those around us immensely. Unforgiveness creates bitterness that not only cripples us, but it also spills into the environment around us affecting those whom we claim to be at peace with. We sometimes underestimate our emotions, failing to realize that how we feel on the inside flows outward and either beautifies or poisons our environment. This could have the innocent paying for the offenses of others.

There is something special that happens to us when we choose to forgive. We become free: free to live, free to love, free to be whom God has called us to be. Have you ever noticed that when you harbor unforgiveness and bitterness you are usually not yourself, especially when around the offender? You tread carefully, always on edge, and building a wall of defense. However, this is not God's will for us. He wants us to live freely.

In this book, we are going to explore what it means to be hurt, its impact on those hurt, the offender, the society at large and especially its impact on our relationship with God, our creator.

Chapter 1
THE STRUGGLE WITHIN

The hardest part about going through difficult challenges is the knowledge that someone else could be responsible for it. It is much harder to go through the pain if this certain someone is a loved one, family, close friend, or a person you have chosen to open your heart to. Managing human emotions is complicated and if mismanaged, could lead to more pain which could result in bitterness. The human heart has the capacity to take one situation and present multiple variations, perspectives, and truths. This is why the Bible makes it clear that we must work hard to secure our hearts. It advises us to guard it with all diligence. In essence, we should make protecting our hearts a priority. You must consciously make a decision to be selective about what you allow into your heart and what you allow to take root in you.

Forgiveness: The Struggle

> Keep thy heart with all diligence;
> for out of it are the issues of life.
> —Proverbs 4:23

Another way to phrase this would be, the issues of life flow out of the heart. Therefore, anything that impacts your life and directs your responses must first take root in your heart. This means that you need to protect yourself by choosing not to let garbage in. Remember, "junk in = junk out."

The human heart is so frail and often prone to error. It takes a lot of hard work and prayer to get to a place of constant readiness to forgive others and let go. That is why no human being can form healthy, balanced, and long-lasting relationships without God and His love. A combination of His love and generous affection is what helps us through it all. This is what makes it possible for us to overlook how others have wronged us and focus more on our need to forgive the offense and move on from it. It also opens our eyes to our contribution towards the situation.

> For God so loved the world, that he gave his only begotten Son, that

> whosoever believeth in him should
> not perish, but have everlasting life.
> —JOHN 3:16

As long as we have breath in our nostrils, offenses will come and if we are not careful, we will end up holding on to them. This might in turn prevent us from forging forward and building our relationship with God.

> Then said he unto the disciples, it is impossible but that offences will come: but woe unto him, through whom they come!
> —LUKE 17:1

We are imperfect. We do not wake up in the morning thinking, "How can I be offensive today?" We unfortunately get carried away in the fragility of our hearts and emotions and end up doing things to hurt even the people we love the most. Instead of believing people are out to hurt you, train your heart to see their motives through the eyes of God. God gives people the benefit of love and grace. Be flexible enough to extend grace, love, and mercy towards others like Jesus would. Practicing this consistently will

Forgiveness: The Struggle

help you become more comfortable with forgiving others and moving on because you will not allow yourself to take offense on the matter.

Unforgiveness puts us in a place of conflict with God. The Bible makes it clear that God forgives us as we forgive others (Mark 11:25–26). The enemy knowing this gives us reasons why we should not forgive others just so we can become distant from God and unable to commune freely with Him. Managing unforgiveness is not easy. Sometimes you think you have forgiven and moved on, only to realize later that it's not quite so. You do all you can to rid yourself of the pain and the memories. You try to eliminate the guards you have put up against that person. There is a saying that goes, "once bitten, twice shy," which means, in an attempt to protect our hearts and prevent reoccurrences of actions we found unpleasing, we build fences. But when you truly love God and are in touch with His spirit, something inside of you nudges and reminds you to reassess yourself and your heart to ensure you have truly forgiven.

The Struggle Within

You assess and reassess, you adjust and readjust as needed and yet, this thing would not resolve itself. You know why? Because you do not have the power to resolve it, correct it, release it, or make it go away. Only the Lord Jesus has that power and ability to help you feel better. The great thing about that is that He wants to do it for you and in you if only you would let Him in and release it all at His feet. Now you ask, how do I release it? It is in the same way you confess with your mouth and believe in your heart that Jesus is Lord.

> That if thou shalt confess with thy mouth the Lord Jesus, and shalt believe in thine heart that God hath raised him from the dead, thou shalt be saved.
> —Romans 10:9

You confess the pain or hurt with your mouth to the hearing of Christ Jesus and you decide in your heart to let go of it. Then commit it to the Lord Jesus in prayer and ask Him to help you through it and to strengthen your heart. Once you have successfully done this, if done right, you should feel some relief.

Forgiveness: The Struggle

You then make a move of conflict resolution with the individual who hurt you.

> Therefore if thou bring thy gift to the altar, and there rememberest that thy brother hath ought against thee; Leave there thy gift before the altar, and go thy way; first be reconciled to thy brother, and then come and offer thy gift.
> —Matthew 5:23–24

This step is important because God will not accept your gift to Him (prayer, time, resource etc.) until you have forgiven those who hurt you. In the Bible passage above, Jesus asks us to go find our offender and make peace. You must bring yourself closure by having an open conversation with your offender. Avoiding it does not make it go away. Speak to him or her; pour out your heart, your hurt, and your pain. By doing so, you not only release yourself, but you also give the other person an opportunity to be released and to reflect on how he or she contributed to the situation. Shockingly, you may find that you were mistaken all along or might have overreacted.

The Struggle Within

Please note that this candid conversation is not equivalent to the words spoken in anger or during a heated argument. Often when we are angry, we say things we do not mean and interpret things in ways not intended.

I would like to take a moment to address abusive relationships, as there might not be an opportunity to have an honest, open conversation with the offender. If you have found yourself in such a relationship, please know that is it not your fault. God expects us to love each other both within the context of marriage and in all other relationships in our lives. He did not intend for any man or woman to dominate or oppress each other.

> And God said, Let us make man in our image, after our likeness: and let them have dominion over the fish of the sea, and over the fowl of the air, and over the cattle, and over all the earth, and over every creeping thing that creepeth upon the earth. So God created man in his *own* image, in the image of God created he him; male and female created he them. And God blessed them, and God said unto them, Be fruitful, and

multiply, and replenish the earth, and subdue it: and have dominion over the fish of the sea, and over the fowl of the air, and over every living thing that moveth upon the earth.
—Genesis 1:26–28

As you can see in the scriptures, God gave us dominion over animals and plants, not over other human beings.

If you are in an abusive relationship or have experienced abuse, please remember that it is not your fault and that the other person chose to be abusive. It is his or her problem and this person needs to come to the realization of their poor choices and should seek help. You should not remain in an abusive relationship. Please take steps to break free. Also, please note that you may not be able to reason with an abusive individual in order to help him or her see how their actions have hurt you. Do not fault yourself for that.

You can still heal from all the pain and hurt with the help of God and a support system. Please seek help. It might be a good idea to speak to a professional counselor who can help you process the emotions. Speak openly to God about how you are feeling and how much you are hurting. Ask Him to heal your heart, grant you peace, and to help you find yourself in Him.

If you are reading this book and you have been abusive towards others, please know that you are not beyond redemption. The Lord Jesus loves you and He wants to heal and deliver you. He wants to form a relationship with you and give you a new beginning. At the end of this book, there is a simple prayer you can say in order to give your heart to Jesus and allow Him to begin the healing process in you.

Pain or No Pain, You Must Still Forgive

When God asks us to forgive, His intention is not to minimize our emotions, our hurt, or our pain. He just wants us, despite the hurt, to forgive and let go as our destiny with Him is at stake if we do not.

Think about it: If God does not forgive your sins because you could not forgive an offender, then you stay separated from Him.

If you remain separated from Him, you cannot fulfill the life He has ordained for you.

> But if ye forgive not men their trespasses, neither will your Father forgive your trespasses.
> —MATTHEW 6:15

> Behold, the Lord's hand is not shortened, that it cannot save; neither his ear heavy, that it cannot hear: But your iniquities have separated between you and your God, and your sins have hid his face from you, that he will not hear.
> —ISAIAH 59:1–2

This means that it is okay to hurt and cry if we must, but after doing so, *we still must forgive*. Sometimes, unbeknown to us, our emotions get the best of us and make us believe that our pain is too deep, too real, and too uncomfortable to confront. But the truth is unless you are willing to confront your pain, the responsibility to forgive becomes very difficult and almost impossible. For true forgiveness and healing to occur, you must be willing

The Struggle Within

to go through the process and sort out your emotions with the help of the Holy Spirit.

Forgiveness is not a one-time deal. You must choose to forgive over and over again. Sometimes, you have forgiven but you find yourself reliving the pain and the hurt all over again. This is not a reflection on your willingness to forgive, it just proves what the scriptures says about casting down every thought and imagination contrary to the knowledge of God. In essence, do not hold yourself captive to your struggle with forgiveness.

God knows that it will take time, practice, and above all, His grace. Your job is to not give up and to keep leaning on the help the Lord Jesus so richly supplies.

> For the weapons of our warfare are not carnal, but mighty through God to the pulling down of strong holds.
> —2 Corinthians 10:4

When the enemy tries to tell you that you cannot forgive, remember that forgiveness is a process. Your response should be, "The Lord rebukes you, Satan. I have forgiven and will continue to forgive." Sometimes, you may have to wake up every day forgiving the same person all over again and that is okay. This should not discourage you, neither should it make you feel like you are not making progress. Instead, encourage yourself that you are strong for getting up every day and making a decision to forgive all over again. Speak it out loud and mean it with your heart. As you commit your heart and your mind to forgiving, eventually your spirit and soul will catch on.

Chapter 2
DEALING WITH DIFFICULT PEOPLE

Let us look at how we can best manage relationships with people who have challenging personalities. You need these people in order to grow. If you shield yourself from everyone who could potentially offend or hurt you, how can you identify your own strengths, weaknesses, and opportunities for growth? These are skills that can make you better prepared for the kingdom of God.

The philosophy of "once bitten twice shy" is the way of the world and does not apply in God's formula. God is not asking us to be foolish but have a heart large enough to accommodate others and their excesses. If you choose to push people away after they have hurt you, then you are choosing not to grow.

I struggled once with someone in my life who had hurt me one time too many and I decided that the best way for me to protect myself was to avoid this individual and have little or nothing to do with her. To my greatest enlightenment, the Holy Spirit would not let me do that. He explained to me that if I avoided everyone who had hurt me at some point, I will not grow into a healthy Christian. His explanation was that the only way for me to truly learn forgiveness was to continually interact with this individual as that would teach my heart to love more generously and to extend grace to others, even in their weakest moments. What an amazing lesson I learned in that season. It was not easy to do but it was necessary. Because I was willing and opened up my heart, He gave me the strength and grace to continue to forgive her. Eventually my heart healed, and I was able to move past the hurt.

> Then came Peter to him, and said, Lord, how oft shall my brother sin against me, and I forgive him? till seven times? Jesus saith unto him, I say not unto thee, Until seven times: but, Until seventy times seven."
> —MATTHEW 18:21–22

You must relate with people who have hurt you badly. Our Lord Jesus says that we will be hurt seventy multiplied by seven times a day, making a total of four hundred and ninety times a day and His expectation is that we forgive each time and keep loving. Let's be real: love is the key to the kingdom of God and the key to the heart of God. Love is what compelled God to send Jesus to the cross. He makes it clear that we might have all manners of gifts but if we lack love, it is all of no use.

> Though I speak with the tongues of men and of angels, and have not charity, I am become as sounding brass, or a tinkling cymbal. And though I have the gift of prophecy, and understand all mysteries, and all knowledge; and though I have all faith, so that I could remove mountains, and have not charity, I am nothing. And though I bestow all my goods to feed the poor, and though I give my body to be burned, and have not charity, it profiteth me nothing.
>
> —1 CORINTHIANS 13:1–3

Forgiveness: The Struggle

We sometimes categorize certain individuals as "difficult to love" but the fact is God expects us to still love them. He is very clear that if we lack love, then we have nothing. Love is what differentiates you as a child of God. It is the language and the culture of God's kingdom. I remember a few years ago, the Holy Spirit asked me to fast and wait on Him. I simply obeyed, not knowing what I was fasting about.

At about 6:00 p.m. or so on the day of my fast, I remember being in my car driving back home when I said to Him, "You still have not told me why I am fasting."

He spoke ever so gently into my spirit saying, "I want to teach you how to love."

Sensing what seemed to be a contradiction, I responded, "But I already know how to love."

"No you don't," He said, "and I want to teach you."

Years later, I am so grateful that He chose to make that investment in me because He really taught my heart how to love others. He has taught me what it means to be generous with love, and how to be gracious towards others. He has also taught me how to curtail

Dealing with Difficult People

my flesh so I can always find my way in Him to forgive others and to let go of offenses. To be sincere, the experience of each offense is different. I have learned that the ease to forgive depends on a few things like the nature of offense, what happened and by whom; but all in all, God has been faithful. He has given my heart such elasticity. With His help and guidance, my heart expresses love and grace towards others, even in times that I have felt deeply hurt.

You need "difficult people" in your life to help test the strength of your love cord. You cannot say that you truly love others and are generous with forgiveness without it being tested. Relating constantly with those that have offended you without any reservations in your heart is proof that your love bank is intact. Does this mean you need to be best friends with them? Not exactly, but it does mean that you have to be comfortable enough to be able to relate with them from a place of authenticity, love, and respect. Do not become a victim of memorized offenses and hurts, especially concerning those with whom you have built a monumental friendship. Choose to let go. Allow God to help free your heart.

> Recompense to no man evil for evil. Provide things honest in the sight of all men.
> If it be possible, as much as lieth in you, live peaceably with all men.
> —ROMANS 12:17–18

> Finally, brethren, farewell. Be perfect, be of good comfort, be of one mind, live in peace; and the God of love and peace shall be with you.
> —2 CORINTHIANS 13:11

The Bible admonishes not to repay evil for evil. Many times, we are tempted to respond to people the exact same way they behaved towards us, but the Lord Jesus encourages us to respond differently. He wants us to express His love, even to those who are undeserving. When it is hardest to love, we need to seek Him and ask for grace to love. Jesus is the reconciler of life. He is the one who extends grace towards us all. Through Him, we can do all things including love those who are difficult to love.

> Then departed Barnabas to Tarsus, for to seek Saul: And when he had found him, he brought him unto Antioch. And it came to pass, that a whole year they assembled themselves with the church, and taught much people. And the disciples were called Christians first in Antioch.
> —Acts 11:25–26

Chapter 3
HOW DO I HEAL?

*P*ain is real. The hurt we feel when we think we have been betrayed, disrespected, or insulted by others really stings. We must, however, make up our minds to release the hurt and the individuals who are responsible for causing the pain in the first place. The great news about the work Jesus did for us on Calvary and the great work He continues to do is that it enables us to enjoy His grace to do all things.

> I can do all things through Christ which strengtheneth me.
> —Philippians 4:13

That being said, I would like to set the record straight. You cannot truly heal without going through. Avoidance does not bring healing. Although it may mask the situation for a while, the rawness of all that occurred is nicely buried under the mask. The day the mask comes off, all the hurt, pain and emotions which have been nicely tucked away will come spilling out. The true way to resolve hurt is to go through it. No one truly heals by wishing the pain away, or by pretending that it never happened. You must allow yourself to process the pain that comes with learning to forgive and letting go for the glory of God.

True healing does not occur unless you go through the situation, deal with the pain, and sort through the emotions. This sometimes means talking or crying it through with the offender or a trusted companion. The key point here is *you must work through the pain*. Remember that burying an emotion or hurt does not help you heal. You might think it is healed but it has not. All you have done is create a scab over it. Anytime you hit the scab with another offense, it breaks open and the wound remains fresh. This means you relive the pain all over again. Sometimes, it could be worse than before. Your failure to properly deal with the issues wears your tolerance thin and places so much demand on your heart that if care is not taken, your heart might harbor too much pain or bitterness.

Difference Between a Scab and a Scar

Just like a physical wound, whenever a conflict occurs, it could lead to a wound and form a scab over it while it heals on the inside. If healthy healing occurs, the scab is eaten away slowly, and eventually, a scar is formed. When the scab is not allowed to serve its purpose of protecting the wound bed during the healing process, it eventually opens up again without the wound being properly healed.

A scab hurts. It hurts because the wound underneath it is still fresh. My daughter sustained a wound to her knee during a fall at school. The healing process began, and a scab formed over the wound. A few days later, while in the shower, she scrubbed the knee a bit too hard and the scab fell off, making the wound raw again and causing her to feel the same pain she felt when she first got injured.

Do you know that the same happens to us whenever we do not allow our emotional wounds to heal properly? Many of us unfortunately keep pulling the scab off our emotional wounds by recounting the details of what occurred. We fail to give the wound time so it can properly heal. Every time you recount hurtful experiences, you relive the pain.

Leave the past alone. Allow offenses to go. Allow them to roll off your back and stop picking at the details of the event. Your inability to stop talking or brooding over it, keeps the wound fresh, prevents it from healing, and keeps it very much alive. One of the steps to forgiveness is to stop talking and thinking about the offense.

Unless a wound is fully healed, it does not become a scar. It remains fresh underneath a scab which is supposed to serve as a temporary covering of protection, so the wound gets the chance to heal properly. It is unfortunate that quite a number of people never truly heal, therefore, the wound remains scabbed for years at a time. At the slightest provocation, the scab falls off and the rawness and pain of the wound is experienced all over again. Some people have tried to confront their pain but because it hurts too much, they walked away from dealing with it and attempt to carry on with life as though the pain does not exist. This is not God's will for us.

How Do I Heal?

> If it be possible, as much as lieth in you, live peaceably with all men.
> —ROMANS 12:18

Can you imagine having a physical wound and you keep pulling the scab off repeatedly? It will not heal as intended and will cause a lot of discomfort and pain. Unfortunately, many of us keep pulling the scab off our emotional wounds and will not allow them to truly heal. If, however, you allow the scab to go through due process, the wound underneath will eventually heal. During the scab period, the wound is being fed by the body with the proper nutrients and blood cells required to facilitate its healing. If these items are absent, the wound will not be able to heal properly. Likewise, your emotional hurt or pain requires certain nutrients and attributes in order to heal properly. The Holy Spirit serves as the scab when we sustain emotional wounds. He does this by attempting to shield your heart and emotions to allow room for some solitude within the wound bed (your heart) that promotes healing and restoration. Sometimes we won't allow the process to occur as He had intended. We keep poking at the wound, reliving the graphics in our minds and hearts, recounting our experience without understanding that the healing we seek will not come until we lay it all to rest in His care and grace.

> And grieve not the Holy Spirit of God, whereby ye are sealed unto the day of redemption.
> —Ephesians 4:30

Unfortunately, some of us are still walking around with open wounds. We have refused to confront the pain and resolve it, thereby no scabs, no scars.

You see, the Holy Spirit is your covering. He is your seal until Jesus returns for His church. Allow Him take care of you and seal you up from pain and suffering. Stop pushing Him away because it feels good to have others feel sorry for you. Allow the Holy Spirit to do what Jesus asked Him to do in your life. Jesus promised when He was leaving the Earth, that He was not leaving us without comfort, help, or direction. Jesus said He was leaving us with the Holy Spirit so He can guide us concerning all things. Allow the Holy Spirit to guide and help guard your heart against the venom of pain that threatens to hold you bound.

> But the Comforter, which is the Holy Ghost, whom the Father will send in my name, he shall teach you all things, and bring all things to your remembrance, whatsoever I have said unto you.
> —JOHN 14:26

The Holy Spirit is the scab and every time you brood over and recount the hurt, you disregard Him, thereby pulling the scab off.

Unlike a scab, a scar is a reminder of the wound but without the pain attached to the wound. It reminds you that you experienced something painful, but the emotion attached to it does not exist. It signifies a wound that has healed properly and more so, scars fade away overtime. This is the forgetting piece of true forgiveness. God expects us to live our lives as scar free as possible by resolving issues effectively and timely. Allow Him to help us to forget over time. Just as you would not want a scar on your physical self, emotional scars are not pretty either and should be allowed to fade away.

Chapter 4
WORKING THROUGH IT

What does it mean then to work through your hurt or pain? First, you must acknowledge that the offense occurred, and you must be open to understanding the events that led to it. Things are not always the way they appear. Open your heart to understand not just how the offense made you feel but the heart of the person that offended you. I promise that this is not always easy to do but you can if you are determined enough to stop carrying a baggage of hurt around. Secondly, make a decision to let go, not only because of the other person, but because you owe it to yourself. You need to forgive others so you can feel free and enjoy peace within.

> Take the time not only to understand your pain but to also understand the heart of the offender.

Deuces

This street slang means "peace." We must always be positioned in a place of peace. We should be eager to diffuse situations and not so readily take offense at the actions of others. Empathy, they say is putting yourself in the shoes of another.

I have a beloved sister who once was ill but was unwilling to share how she was truly feeling and what was going on with her. I was worried about her health but also found myself almost taking offense at the fact she was unwilling to share what was going on so I would know how to help and support her. But I thank God for the Holy Spirit who quickly corrected me by pointing out that it was not about me and that she was the one who was ill and needed all the love and support she could get. He made it clear to me

Working Through It

that my role at the moment was that of love and support and nothing else. I had no place to be upset or offended by her but instead I should pray for her and seek opportunities to let her know that she is loved. It was a "wow" moment for me.

We sometimes take offense at the actions of others. If we can think back and take inventory of our lives and actions, we can then see how we have possibly failed others in a similar manner.

I work as a nurse leader and I remember a few years ago, one of my nurses requested for a transfer through the human resources (HR) department to another unit without my knowledge. After the transfer was approved, I received an email from HR alerting me that she had been accepted by the new department and asked me for a release date. I suddenly got quite offended as I thought to myself that she did not even tell me she was applying to a new department so that I could have better prepared myself to recruit for a replacement. As this thought went through my mind and anger began to rise within me, I heard the Holy Spirit say, "Why are you angry? You did the exact same thing to your boss when you applied to a different position without her knowledge." I immediately became humbled and apologized for being upset with my nurse and graciously responded to HR with a release date. I learned a great lesson that day. Many of the offenses we hold against others, we have also been guilty for at some point in our lives. In essence, before we decide to take offense by the actions of others, we ought to remember that just like us, they are human and are capable of making mistakes.

The Work

Unless you work through your emotions and your pain, you cannot truly heal and move past it. A buried emotion and a dead emotion are very different from each other. Something buried can be resurrected to life again under the right circumstance and situation. When something is dead, it is lifeless and has no opportunity to breathe or come back to life. It loses breath, life, and power. When your pain truly dies, it loses the ability to cause you hurt. Forgiveness renders the pain powerless over you and others.

Do you know your pain does not only affect you? It affects everything and everyone around you.

Pain is crippling and it prevents you from being the best version of yourself.

After you have confronted your emotions and feelings, you then must release it to God through the Holy Spirit by asking Him to take the lead and help heal your heart. Remember, He is the scab over your wound and only He has the ability to truly help you heal adequately. Hand it over to Him in the place of prayer. Speak openly to Him about how the events made you feel and honestly tell Him to help your heart and take the pain away. It may not happen automatically, but your persistence and willingness will help over time.

> O Lord, thou hast searched me, and known me. Thou knowest my downsitting and mine uprising, thou understandest my thought afar off. Thou compassest my path and my lying down, and art acquainted with all my ways. For there is not a

word in my tongue, but, lo, O Lord,
thou knowest it altogether.
—Psalm 139:1–4

God cares about you and sees your pain. He is always ready to hear you and to see you through. His loves for you extends far beyond your natural understanding. Do not hesitate to call upon Him and trust in Him.

Do Some Offenses Hurt More Than Some?

You bet they do.

Those closest to you tend to cause you the greatest pain and affliction. This is not because their offense is greater; it is simply because you hold them to a higher standard. You subconsciously have expectations, that they will never hurt you. This in itself is unfair because they are human just like you are. They are not perfect. As long as they remain in the flesh, they are prone to causing offense. They have the potential to hurt you, not because they do not love you as much as you love them, but because they are simply human.

Managing Offenses When They Are Least Expected

Have you ever been offended by someone you least expected it from? It usually hurts much more because you expect so much from that individual. You expect more care, more love, better understanding, etc. As humans we are all capable of making mistakes and would sometimes hurt others, even when we do not intend to. We often trust certain people and place them on such a pedestal that an offense from them is very difficult to process and hurts deeply. A lot of us find it particularly challenging to confront and process such offenses because we expect such individuals to know better. It's important to highlight that we have weaknesses and would sometimes offend one another subconsciously. We must learn to readily extend God's grace and mercy toward others, remembering that they are just as frail and as imperfect as we are.

Beware of the mistake of expecting others to behave the way you would. Because you are extremely thoughtful about your actions and reactions does not mean that everyone else will be. Your ability to expect others to respond and behave in the same exact way as you is already a trap set up for that person to disappoint you.

> People are people. They're frail, imperfect, and human so stop expecting "man" to act like "God."

Trust has a way of making you vulnerable, but you cannot afford to use it as an excuse to stay angry and bitter. Joseph trusted his brothers and shared his dreams with them with an open heart, yet they betrayed him (Gen. 37:3–28). He got to Potiphar's house and opened up his heart again to trusting others and was disappointed yet again (Gen. 39:1–20). But do you know the amazing thing about Joseph? He never allowed all the betrayal and pain to make him bitter. He forgave easily and moved on. God being so gracious, He used the same gift of dreams that got him into slavery to find his freedom and fulfil his destiny (Genesis 41).

Then the chief cupbearer said to Pharaoh, "I remember my offenses today. When Pharaoh was angry with his servants and put me and the chief baker in custody in the house of the captain of the guard, we dreamed on the same night, he and I, each having a dream with its own interpretation. A young Hebrew was there with us, a servant of the captain of the guard. When we told him, he interpreted our dreams to us, giving an interpretation to each man according to his dream. And as he interpreted to us, so it came about. I was restored to my office, and the baker was hanged." Then Pharaoh sent and called Joseph, and they quickly brought him out of the pit. And when he had shaved himself and changed his clothes, he came in before Pharaoh. And Pharaoh said to Joseph, "I have had a dream, and there is no one who can interpret it. I have heard it said of you that when you hear a dream you can interpret it." Joseph answered Pharaoh, "It is not in me; God will give Pharaoh a favorable answer."

—GENESIS 41:9–16, ESV

Many of us have unfortunately shut down our gifts, talents, and callings because of pain inflicted upon us by others. Can you imagine if he had abandoned the gift and his ability to be there for others because of his pain? He would have died in prison and never fulfilled his God ordained purpose and destiny. Learn from Joseph and do not allow others to derail you by holding you down with unforgiveness and bitterness. There are many individuals walking around the Earth who have given up on whom God created them to be because someone has hurt them, disrespected them or took advantage of them. Do not allow the enemy to do that to you. Remember the enemy only comes to steal, kill, and destroy.

> The thief cometh not, but for to steal, and to kill, and to destroy: I am come that they might have life, and that they might have it more abundantly.
>
> —JOHN 10:10

Think about how often you have hurt and offended others when you did not mean to. If you are capable of hurting others, even when you have the best intentions, others will sometimes hurt you too without intending to. Now, let us assume the offense was intentional. Your response needs to be the same, not so much for the offender but for yourself. Let us be clear, it is true that the Bible says that "to whom much is given, much is expected...." (Luke 12:48). We must however position ourselves to look beyond the weaknesses and imperfections of others.

Your ease in forgiving others is actually a sign of personal, spiritual, and emotional growth.

Here are a few questions you could ask yourself to help you process offenses:

1. Was the offense intentional?
2. Did the person purposefully mean to cause me harm?

3. If this individual knew better, would he or she have chosen differently?
4. Could I have offended another in the same manner?
5. Do I expect others to forgive me when I hurt them?
6. Do I expect forgiveness from God for the many times I offend Him?

If you answered "yes" to any of the questions, then you would have reminded yourself that as you are human, others are too. We are flawed individuals, so offense is inevitable. If you can see just how imperfect you are as a human, it is only right that you extend others the same courtesy. Since offense is virtually unavoidable, what you do with it and how you choose to process offense is really what matters.

Choose love over hate. Choose forgiveness over malice.

I am learning that love is never about the other person. It is always about you and sometimes you may not get back the love that you give. If you fail to realize that love is your agent to freedom and your permission to live life without resentments and grudges, you may compromise and choose to love less because it is easier to love only those who love you. *Unbeknown to us, love un-multiplied becomes deactivated. The less you love, the harder it becomes to love.*

We do not extend love because humans are perfect. That is so far from the truth. The reason to love is simply that God ordained it and requires it of us.

> A new commandment I give unto you, That ye love one another; as I have loved you, that ye also love one another.
>
> —JOHN 13:34

According to 1st Corinthians 13:1, love is not self-seeking. Love is not "me first." Love cares more for others than self and is always demonstrated by selfless commitment on behalf of another. So, whenever you choose to love others in spite of how you are feeling, you demonstrate the word of God. I love because I love God and want to please Him, not because the people love me back. Love, through Christ Jesus, helps you see every person as half-full, not half-empty. It helps you focus on what is great, right, and positive about that person and not what is wrong or imperfect. This is another dimension of honor: to see the good in someone, value their difference, and acknowledge the unique way they were created and fashioned.

It becomes much easier to forgive wrongs because you love. Your ability to love does not always guarantee that you will be understood. In fact, the harder and more purely you love, the greater the likelihood of you being misunderstood. The reason for this is that the world is skeptical of pure love and struggles with comprehending that a person can love another without an underlying motive. This phenomenon is one I find very odd because people often yearn for love but when it shows up, they are so suspicious of it that is sometimes mismanaged and abused. Why? Because the devil thrives in hate and malice and in an attempt to control humanity, he emphasizes hate and skepticism over true love, mercy, and grace.

Unveiling the Real Enemy

> For we wrestle not against flesh and blood, but against principalities, against powers, against the rulers of the darkness of this world, against spiritual wickedness in high places.
> —Ephesians 6:12

The Bible makes it clear that we wrestle not against flesh and blood but against powers and spiritual wickedness in high places. There is a spiritual force behind every experience. Positive experiences are sponsored spiritually by God while negative experiences are sponsored by the devil. Every time you go through something, remember that nothing just happens. There is a spiritual sponsor or influence behind the experience. The problem is that because we do not see this spiritual influence, we tend to forget or not realize that it exists. The enemy of our souls, Satan, is a master of disguise. He is good at making things appear the way they are not. He wraps wickedness in a fancy package and presents it as something else.

Whenever you feel any emotion, there is a spiritual sponsor behind that emotion. When someone offends you, you must remember to recognize the enemy in the situation. Understand that all Satan seeks is an opportunity to gain access into your life. He does this by making you vulnerable. Sin makes you vulnerable to the enemy and gives him legal right to wreak havoc in your life. Unforgiveness, unresolved anger, malice and hatred are forms of sin that could grant satan access into your life. So, when that person hurts you deeply, remember that the entire situation was sponsored by the enemy. He continues to propagate his wickedness by hardening your heart to forgive, only so he can have his way. Do not be ignorant of his devices. Remember that he comes to steal, kill, and destroy, and nothing more (John 10:10).

Most recently God told me that I should not be a partaker of the sins of others.

> Lay hands suddenly on no man, neither be partaker of other men's sins: keep thyself pure.
> —1 Timothy 5:22

He told me that because someone else chooses to misbehave is no reason for me to choose to misbehave as well. God said to me that not forgiving the individual makes me a partaker of that person's sin. If my pain is that another individual has sinned by hurting me, is it proper that I respond by sinning against God as well because I chose not to forgive?

Remember that for every thought that crosses your mind, there is a spiritual influence and you must choose wisely whose influence you accept.

> Know ye not, that to whom ye yield yourselves servants to obey, his servants ye are to whom ye obey; whether of sin unto death, or of obedience unto righteousness?
> —Romans 6:16

How Do I Know I Have Not Gotten over an Offense?

- When you have changed who you are to avoid being hurt again
- When you cannot relate normally with the offender

To you who frequently like to offend and do not know how to appreciate and value the people in your life, I want you to know that the only reason you can hurt them is because they have placed value on you.[1] They have placed value on the relationship they have with you and if you cannot honor that value then you are indirectly saying, "Take the value you have placed upon me away." When someone who loves you says to you, "What you have done or said hurts me," it is your responsibility to look at the situation and make amends as needed. If you fail to, that person may withdraw the power you have been given to hurt them in an attempt to protect themselves from more harm. Once this happens, you begin to lose the affection they have for you as well.

> Did you not know, that the Amygdala which is a part of the Limbic System in the brain helps us process painful emotions and also helps us love? So, you cannot have one without the other. Be careful the way you treat and respond to those who love you.[2]

Chapter 5
RESOLVE OR EVADE

The avoidance of an individual is not forgiveness. When you feel at ease and comfortable about someone who has offended you as long as you do not see him or her, this is not forgiveness. True forgiveness is attained when you see the individual and you feel comfortable relating. It does not mean you have to be best of friends, but you must enjoy maximum comfort levels relating with and conversing with such person.

Do you know that even in situations where someone maliciously hurts you, God still expects you to forgive? Once a colleague at work offended me by saying damaging words about my character to other colleagues. When I found out, I was deeply hurt, and it took a very intense conversation to help others understand that what was reported was not true. I felt so bad about the situation that I decided to avoid my offender. But one day

Forgiveness: The Struggle

God made it clear to me in the place of prayer that He is my protector and defender. If He is the One who fights for me, then why do I allow the excuse of distrust to keep me in a state of disobedience to Him. If He is the one who fights for me and protects me, then my priority should be living my life in total obedience to Him always, so I can remain in continued fellowship with Him.

Similar to avoidance, deflection does not resolve issues effectively either. Sometimes, in an attempt to free ourselves of pain and hurt, we project the pain onto others. We confront the issue with them but with the intention of making them feel the pain we felt or even make them feel guilty. This is wrong if your goal is to free then it should be your joy that others are free from every emotional pain and torment. The truth be told, someone else's guilt about an offense they committed does not lighten your burden. Seek godly ways to make peace and reach a resolution.

Resolve or Evade

Beware of Defense Mechanisms

Defense mechanisms protect the individual putting them up, not the relationship. It is selfish and unfair. As compared to working through the emotions and helping each other be better, you decide to shut one person out. This act makes relationships worse. Building up emotional walls separates the people involved. Remember, walls do not only keep things out, they also stop things from going in. This means that if you build walls in an attempt to protect yourself from getting hurt, what you are doing is also rejecting love, care, and support. You will overthink situations and give a meaning to everything being said to you based on your past experiences with that individual. Sometimes, you could be wrong. When no harm is intended, you expect harm and respond on the defense, leaving the person trying to communicate with you confused and frustrated. It is as though he or she is trying to be better, but you fail to give an opportunity for that to actually happen. If care is not taken, a person who loves and cares about you deeply gives up on you and walks out of your life.

Stop expecting people to be like you. We are very different from one another. The earlier we start recognizing and appreciating everyone's differences, the better for us all.

Resolving Conflicts

It is very important that conflicts are resolved in real time. This must happen in order to prevent further and more permanent damage. Most of us underestimate the power of the phrase, "I am sorry." We sometimes think it carries no weight or that apologizing is an admittance of guilt, but this is not true. Saying "I am sorry" simply means I acknowledge you are hurting; that's all. You may not even understand the reason for the hurt but because you perceive the hurt or that the hurt was verbalized to you; you are willing to apologize. This serves as a sign of respect and concern for the other person's emotional health.

> **Conflicts not resolved timely will create wounds.**

> Let nothing be done through strife or vainglory; but in lowliness of mind let each esteem other better than themselves.
> —PHILIPPIANS 2:3

If you were the one hurting, you would not want the one inflicting the pain to keep justifying his or her actions or trying to exonerate him or herself. I am sure all you would need and appreciate is an acknowledgement of your pain and a sincere apology. Simply saying, "I hear you, I understand, and I am sorry for hurting you. That was not my intention" most likely will be the first step to completely resolving the conflict.

> **Be mindful of the way you treat and respond to others and remember that everyone wants to be loved and respected.**

The Outlet

As humans, we always feel a need to talk to someone when we are hurting. We feel a need to pour out our hearts, a need to have a listening ear. An outlet in itself is very much helpful but can be damaging if the wrong outlet is chosen. When you talk to me about your pain, I have a responsibility to make sure that you walk away from me feeling better. Anything short of that screams out "wrong outlet." If you get the beautiful opportunity of serving as an outlet to someone else, please ensure that they walk away from you feeling better than they came. Your focus should be on softening their hearts and helping them understand the heart of the offender as much as you possibly can. Please do not spend the amazing opportunity highlighting the wrongdoing and throwing a pity party for the offended.

Chapter 6
TO FORGET OR NOT TO FORGET

What does it really mean when someone says to you after you have been deeply hurt to "forgive and forget?" Many of us pride ourselves in our ability to forgive but not forget. We forgive until the next time the offender hurts us again. From that point, we begin to dig up old emotions, pain, and hurt. These things come rushing in, flooding our minds, making it more challenging to "forgive" this time around. That is why sometimes in relationships we sever ties because "we can't take it anymore." Why? Too many unresolved issues, unforgotten pain, and unprocessed emotions. That is why it is too important to work through your pain, your hurt, and your emotions in real time. God's intention for us is that we behave like Him at all times. He said He forgives us but that is not the end of it, He also forgets our sins. He expects us to do the same with the sins others commit against us.

> For I will be merciful to their unrighteousness, and their sins and their iniquities will I remember no more.
> —Hebrews 8:12

God forgives us and forgets our sins and expects us to be just like Him.

Forgetting does not mean you do not remember you were hurt; it simply means you choose to detach the hurtful emotions from the memory of the event. You choose to forget the pain you experienced as a result of what happened. As you intentionally do this with God's help, you will eventually find that the details of the actual event will start to blur out.

Holding on to the pain keeps the wound fresh. The pain stops you from truly healing and recovering from what happened. If every time you remember the event you still cry, get angry, or feel sad, then you are still living in the moment of that pain. We sometimes think forgetting is foolishness. The enemy tells us that we should remember so we can protect ourselves from getting hurt again in the future. The truth is none of us can truly protect ourselves. Our protection is only guaranteed in God.

The enemy tries all he can to keep you in the realness of the pain. His intention is for the pain to become a prison that keeps you captive, but God's intention is for you to be free. Jesus said He came to give us life and to give it in abundance (John 10:10). Please be careful not to allow the enemy to release the toxicity of pain into your life. Let go of the pain, let go of the emotions, and watch yourself truly heal from the inside out. A wise saying proclaims that forgiveness is harder than fighting and is a display of great strength. What makes the individual strong is the decision to hold back, resist the urge to fight, and forgive instead. Whenever you choose God's way of doing it, you choose life!

Lastly, know that it is a process for hurt to become malice. It takes you thinking about the hurt repeatedly, dissecting it, hypothesizing the intentions, brooding over it, and allowing it to fester. Extend grace, love, and mercy toward the offender and readily forgive the offense remembering that he or she is as human as you are. By doing this, you are set free.

I am learning that in order to survive, live well, and make it into heaven, forgiveness must become my way of life.

I pray that you will have strength and grace to walk in love and to find the courage to forgive as God would expect you to.

If you have read this book and are thinking, "I do not know Jesus, so what is next?" That's okay. You can receive Jesus into your life right now by saying this simple prayer:

> *Lord Jesus, I come to you today. I know I am a sinner and have been entangled with things that are not good for me. I confess my sins and say that I am sorry for all that I have done wrong. I believe that You are the Son of God and that You gave Your life for me by dying on the cross of Calvary. Please wash me clean by Your precious blood and give me a new heart. Come into my*

heart and live in me. Take my life and make me Your own. Today, I make up my mind to love you and to accept Your love for me. This, I pray, in Jesus's mighty name. Amen.

If you said this prayer, you just accepted Jesus as the God of your life. You are born again. At this point, please find a living church where God's love and holiness is preached. It is important for you to have fellowship with other Christians.

Make it a priority to talk to God every day through prayer. Prayer is a simple dialogue between you and the Lord. You speak to Him like you would a friend.

Lastly, purchase a Bible if you do not already have one. Find a translation that is easy for you to understand and study the word of God, daily. The Bible will equip you with the knowledge needed to live a life that pleases Him.

NOTES

1. Isabella Poggi and Francesca D'Errico, "Feeling Offended: A Blow to Our Image and Our Social Relationships," Front .Psychol., January 17, 2018, https://www.frontiersin.org/articles/10.3389/fpsyg.2017.02221/full.

2. Khan Academy. (2020). Emotions: limbic system. https://www.khanacademy.org/science/health-and-medicine/executive-systems-of-the-brain/emotion-lesson/v/emotions-limbic-system (accessed June 7, 2020).

www.ingramcontent.com/pod-product-compliance
Lightning Source LLC
Chambersburg PA
CBHW071318080526
44587CB00018B/3266